The Departm

THE DEPARTMENT OF LOST WISHES

Henry Normal

Flapjack Press

www.flapjackpress.co.uk

Exploring the synergy between performance and the page

Published in 2018 by Flapjack Press
Salford, Gtr Manchester
www.flapjackpress.co.uk

ISBN 978-1-9996707-1-9

Cover photograph © Richard Davis
All other photographs courtesy of the author

Printed by Imprint Digital
Upton Pyne, Exeter, Devon
imprintdigital.com

Dedicated to Nigel and Sue Kirkwood and Terry and Sarah Kirkwood. Not only my oldest friends but definitely my closest – they only lived next door but one.

I would like to thank Linda Hallam, Paul Neads, Theresa Sowerby, Penny Shepherd and my wife Angela Pell for their help in bringing this collection together.

Contents

The Department of Lost Wishes

The first few pages of her diary are always written neatly

The first few pages of her diary are always written neatly
She is meticulous
First impressions last

Around April she is no longer self-conscious
Her character bursts the confines of set agenda

Summer sees a casual familiarity
Some days she writes a rain storm
Some days life is too close to record

September sees few notes but all highly personal
Her comments becoming cryptic

Somehow she never manages to finish a full year
There is never a conclusion
or an acknowledgement to the nature of her final entry

The last few pages of her diary are always
blank

For Christmas she will treat herself once more
and make a commitment
once again

Love ethic

I've brought you some flowers
I hope you like them

I'm not always so forward on a first date
but I've brought you this as well
I hope you don't mind that I've not wrapped it up
It's an album of photos
showing each of my previous lovers
naked
in bed with me
in various positions
taken at the moment of orgasm
with accompanying audio tapes
and videos of the more recent lovers

And then there's all my family photos
A full itinerary of my life so far
A book of my own quotations
A list of all my friends
their likes and dislikes
and a list of their friends

A twelve volume history of my ancestry
The stuffed corpses of all my dead relatives
and life size wax models
of everyone I've ever met
A report from my doctor
My latest X-rays

All the sperm I've ever produced
stretching back to the beginnings of puberty
and all the urine and faeces I've passed

All the hair cut or shaved from my body
my entire collection of toenail clippings
and the pus squeezed from every boil or spot
All the stale sweat released from my pores

A recent study of my philosophical beliefs
My bank statement
A list of my assets, property
and personal possessions
A detailed career plan for the rest of my life
My star chart
A graph of my biorhythms
A signed photo of my God
An explanation of every conscious
or subconscious thought
I've had since my conception
A written declaration of
my expectations in the event of a relationship
An extensive analysis of
all the things we have in common
A list of questions you may want to ask
together with all possible answers

And finally an itemised account as to
how since its creation
the universe
has brought us to this point

I don't suppose you were expecting flowers

In defence of the latecomer

We are all latecomers
having to pick up the threads
whilst the action continues

hastily snatching titbits of insight
from other latecomers
whose initial source was merely

better informed latecomers
informed by other latecomers
often since departed

The coaster – mighty bastion of civilisation

Sponge saucer
unsung since Chaucer

Mop twixt tea and top
Cup cop to sup up slop

Not a furnishing garnish
A guardian of the varnish
ensuring tables free from tea stain tarnish

Diverter of the drip
Leak-lagging lip

O incredible
semi-porous pedestal

Overflow screen
Go-between
Close friend of Mr Sheen

Simple plot with clever stage
to blot beverage
of whatever age

Wedge against the wet
Ingester of the juicy jet

The fine line against fluid anarchy
Comfort-cushion of the panicky

Epitome of order
The great absorber
Part towel part decorative plate
Absorber the Great

Puppy love – a dog's life?

Whatever happened to little Julie Bowers?
She was classy
I'd never seen anyone so clean
she must have washed every day

Proper leather school satchel
with the straps and buckles and everything
just like in the *Bunty* comics
Not that I read *Bunty* comics
Sometimes I cut out the outfits on the back cover

Luckily around this time I discovered masturbation
so I no longer had to hang from playground equipment
to achieve that pleasant tingling sensation in my groin

But Julie Bowers was above all that
she was classy

She was the kind of girl
who would never fool around behind the library curtains
I was just a scruffy kid with snotty sleeves
and hand-me-downs from an older sister
Our love could never be

She lived in the posh part of the council estate
where the houses had hedges too thick to dive through
She was unattainable
a Goddess

She had the complete set of felt-tip colours
The full range with the light and dark brown

To her jigsaws were fun
She entered all the *Blue Peter* competitions
and she could read *Look and Learn* without faking it

She was something of a playground intellectual
and I respected her mind
though in my weaker moments
I just wanted her to snog me
to a state of total exhaustion

That seductive overbite
the cute turned-up nose
her neat ponytail
and those clean knee length white socks
She knew how to drive a boy wild

Yes
she was classy
Mind you
round our way any girl who ate with her mouth closed
was considered classy

What could I do?
I tried to drown my sorrows in Taunton's cider
but developed chronic flatulence instead
Were these really to be the happiest days of my life?

The poem with no name

In the movie
he rode away into the sunset

but the next day
I saw him shopping
in Tesco

Some check-out
woman gave him a bad time
and he never even shot
her once

Which only
goes to prove
Tesco
isn't like real life
at all

My son the poet

Christopher Marlowe wrote for a living
but before his name was made
what did his family make of it all
cobblers being their trade?

Blake's pop ran a hosiery shop
Burns' pop kept a vegetable crop
None of the great bards ever had
a great poet for a dad

Milton's old man was a scrivener
making whatever scriveners make
Hardy's father was a mason
but without the funny handshake

The Chaucer clan were in wine
not of some long literary line
Great poets it can be said
may be born but never bred

Donne's dad was an ironmonger
Shakespeare senior made gloves
Keats' dad shovelled horse shit
whilst his son wrote of inner loves

Life down the wrong end of a telescope

Is it enough to survive?
To exist though not feel alive?
I crave understanding
but feel like the stand-in
for the pilot of Thunderbird 5

Dear John – the fax

She always put her career first
I guess I should have had a hunch
when at the moment of orgasm once
she called out "let's do lunch"

Heart on a string

You play me like a Yo-yo
Taking me high
then sending me solo

Stingray (real not marionette)

As small hands ride these animated surfboards
rising from the water like toast from a toaster
I am unable to reach out

The seaweed reminds me of mistletoe
at a school disco

I have felt this hesitation before

How could I kiss those lips
still bruised from another's trespass?

There are some things you know without being taught

Even as she leant in to touch
I was in love with her
and this, to me, was not about love
but a ritual mocking its appearance

There's plenty more fish in the sea
I've heard said enough times in
the twenty years since to
reinforce a place
amongst the great clichés of life

These flattened dolphins
Star Trek pancakes
charm with their trust and quirky grace

and I
have learnt to recognise
some fish affect you more than others

The kissing of scar tissue

Invent them
caress them
nurture them
possess them
Build your life around them
Never be found without them
Problems

Appreciate them
wallow in them
drain every last swallow from them
You may have none tomorrow and then
you will have problems

Malevolent to inertia

to jar contentment
to haunt complacency
to bait resignation

to tease the tedious and the comfortable

to taunt the skeletons from the cupboard
to aggravate the thorn in the breast
to dip hands in cold blood

to tweak the upturned nose

to worry the apathetic
to trouble the indifferent
to vex the snug

to play devil to the dull
provoke and pester, nettle and grate
to unsettle, to stimulate

to deign against the grain
to disturb

All comfort is sacred to those lost in the night

Those that solicit
illicit kisses
on the corner of Sackville Street

they too cast silver
to enlist wishes
from the well of tears
of a life incomplete

they too were once children
with promises
tender beneath their feet

CHAPTER ONE:
MAYBE THEY SHOULD TEACH SEX EDUCATION
AT SUNDAY SCHOOL

I spent all my pocket money buying her religious memorabilia
It's not that either of us were particularly religious
Church trips were merely a cheap day out
These gifts were tokens of love; prizes, favours, offerings

Not being able to afford a substantial amount
to demonstrate my passion
I even slipped in a couple of extra non-purchased acquisitions;
religious texts and novelty items
I was stealing from God

On reflection I don't recall receiving any keepsakes in return
However, at the time, I was oblivious to such a technicality
My heart was overflowing with the need to give myself
all of myself and that being not enough, to give more

to sacrifice myself
my every possession, my every principle, my immortal soul
regretting that I only had one immortal soul to give
and that it wasn't bigger

And for what?
For reciprocal worship?
No, this was more than I could hope for
Like asking God himself to budge up a bit

No, unconsciously I had settled for a lesser ambition
I had settled for the chance to be allowed to worship

It's easy to see now I must have upset the spontaneity of the occasion a little, leaping from bed after three and a half minutes' extensive foreplay and rushing to the toilet there to wrestle with a Durex for the better part of an hour, but being inexperienced and easily embarrassed and knowing no better at the time it all seemed perfectly justified.

Once alone in the toilet I fumbled frantically in an effort to don my little passion accessory, my sexual fervour now waning fast due in no small measure to the cold toilet seat, the fact that it was her parents' toilet, the less than romantic atmosphere of the white wood-chip walls and do-it-yourself plumbing, the ever-lengthening gap in our mutual arousal and having tried unsuccessfully to roll the strange accoutrement on the wrong way twice further blunting my ardour and leaving me with a task not dissimilar to stacking custard or trying to thread jelly into a pair of Doc Martens.

When eventually I slipped surreptitiously back under the blankets my sexual initiation re-commenced cautiously. Although I'd taken a keen interest in the theory aspect at school there were still one or two points they were never too specific about in sex education classes.

Not mentioning that the sperm doesn't just disappear but can run back down a girl's leg when she stands up was one. The most important omission as far as I was concerned however was not explaining exactly how long the coitus activity should generally take.

For four hours we hammered away trying to make sure that the job was done right. I didn't want to let on that I wasn't adequately potent and she didn't want to let on that she'd had enough three and a half hours since. All the next day we walked around exhausted and bruised, tender and inflamed, recovering from what felt effectively like a four hour Chinese burn on the genitals.

I marvelled at friends who boasted that they did it every night thinking they must have really suffered.

Is red the colour of passion?

Roses are red
often the dahlia
and after sex
you can include genitalia

Honeymoon on the Marie Celeste

Take care when you're in clover
never to appear too smug
For when your cup runneth over
it's easy to be taken for a mug

Joy v Order

Pure loving
is
All or Nothing

Like the queue for the chippy
outside the ground at Man City

The sacrament of compost

We are the ripeness of fruit
and the concentration of coal
the eagle and the bear
the Zulu and the Navaho

We are the acids
and the spoor
the amoeba
and the dinosaur
our common ancestor
the possibility of nature

All flesh is eaten
all blood sipped
evolution is the Eucharist

We are between
all that was
and all that will
live

The miracle of the atom
smacks the breath
of the dead
into the child
as life begets life
begets life

You never see a bright yellow hearse

The English don't die they just become discreet
You never see a hearse clamped on Harley Street
or parked at a picnic site
near Lovers' Leap

You never see a hearse outside a betting shop
left next to a row of prams
You never see the route to the cemetery
served by special hearse trams

You never see a hearse at a wedding
or on adverts for banks
or a row of hearses at a military parade
behind a squadron of tanks

or outside a nightclub at closing time
with racing stripes down the bonnet
or a hearse at the Motor Show
with dead models draped upon it

You never see a double-decker hearse
or a hearse that's extra wide
or a hearse with 4 or 5 coffins
all crammed up inside

You never see a coffin in a sidecar
for a fanatical ex-biker
or a hearse at a transport café
picking up a hitchhiker

You never see a hearse used for ram-raiding
or a hearse with fluffy dice
or a hearse with a taxi meter
so you can keep an eye on the price

Each hearse is always black and clean and neat
because the English don't die they just become discreet

Feeling by numbers

Feeling by numbers
colouring the spaces

joining the dots
filling the blanks

action replacing emotion
like love by committee

discussing the next meeting
reviewing the minutes

the emotion is passed by
show of hands

Shorts are not like short trousers

Short trousers
were just like long trousers
but shorter

to allow for scabs on your knees

These trousers were always grey
and lined with deep pockets
for keeping conkers
and galleys and bubblegum cards
and boiled sweets
with bits of fluff stuck to them

Today's shorts are not as substantial
Flimsy approximations
worn only for set escapes
when there's an excuse
like sport or on holiday
or occasionally round the house
if summer stays the whole weekend
like summers when we were kids

I remember my first pair of long trousers
They made the scabs on my knees disappear
and my legs instantly grew longer
I was as tall as a grown up
Like a detective
or a secret agent

Who do you want to share your silences?

Who is it quickens your heart
when the phone rings?

Whose company makes you giggle
without the need for drinks?

Who do you dream of
when the firelight is yours?

Whose name do you whisper
behind your bedroom door?

To show how easy it is for a mistake to happen

Hickory Dickory Dock
the mouse ran up the clock
The clock struck one
causing a pre-emptive strike escalating
into all out nuclear attack
Hickory Dickory Dock

About weapons falling into the wrong hands

Mary had a little lamb
She also had a thermonuclear device
the Armageddon Activity Set
new from Fisher Price

Class comment

Humpty Dumpty sat on a wall
Humpty Dumpty had a great fall
All the King's horses and all the King's men
were safely tucked away in underground bunkers

About the effects of nuclear fallout

Mary Mary quite contrary
how does your garden grow?
It doesn't

In a similar vein

I had a little pear tree
and nothing would it bear

Green poem

Green are the English pastures
Green – the jealousy of lovers
Green are the fruit pastels
I always offer to others

Columbus thought the world not in fact round but pear-shaped

In 1492
Columbus sailed the ocean blue
It diminishes not his bravado
he envisaged the world as an avocado

The rhapsody of the florist and the butcher

Amid new life she skips
In death his grip is strong
She gives him her tulips
He gives her his tongue

It was Chris Coupe's last thirty pee, two ten pees, a five pee, two two pees and a one. He could afford all manner of chocolate diversion but he never liked to break a thirty pee. He felt like the man in the film *The Million Pound Note*, except not quite so rich.

Could he last the whole day on thirty pee, could he last past dinnertime? At least whilst he retained his options he was a genuine citizen, a potential consumer, an accepted member of society. The government had been farsighted enough to leave him the incentive of 'Freedom of Choice'.

All the slogans and clichés he'd seen throughout his life passed in front of him; 'from small acorns, money breeds money, speculate to accumulate, many a mickle macs a muckle'. He never understood that last one.

But one thing he knew, thirty pee was hope. He was still in the game. This could be the thirty pee that shook the world. He was the thirty pee, the thirty pee was him, and he was proud of it. In his hunger he was proud. Cold and tired he was proud. He was no longer fighting for himself, he was responsible. He was struggling to keep alive the thirty pee. It was above the pettiness of self, comfort, ambition. This was a crusade for an idea. It was true freedom, true democracy, human rights, everything clean and honest worth defending.

Spend that thirty pee? No way.

Within the month Chris died, fist clenched in defiance around thirty pee, two ten pees, a five pee, two two pees, and a one.

Fig.1 and Fig.2 discuss the value of cold sex

Diagrams don't have headaches
never have a lousy day

are never self-conscious and
are always in perfect shape

Diagrams don't mind sex cold
their sole purpose is to breed

closeness and affection
they don't really need

Diagrams are never hurt
and diagrams never bleed

Love by list

1. You're new to my list of acquaintances
2. Let us list the things we have in common
3. Here is a list of good points I've spotted
4. Here is a list of things for us to say
5. and a list of other lists that will come in handy

6. I love you
7. See under list №6 for response
8. You are not responding correctly
9. Have you read your lists?
10. Here is a list of things you are doing wrong

11. Here is another list
12. You will see some items have been duplicated
13. I'm afraid I've lost the list with your good points
14. but it's ok
15. I'm too busy keeping all these lists together

16. I'm going to have to take you off
17. my list of active relationships
18. Still don't worry I have a list for you
19. We can put you here under
20. failures

A sort of modern Cinderella

Her pen she laid next to mine
round at my pad
Then she ran out this morning
without a line
as indeed her pen had

Was man an afterthought?

He took seven days making of Heaven and Earth
but with his weekend coming up soon
not even God does his best work
on a Saturday afternoon

Cupid's pincushion

Struck from Cupid's bow
my heart is lacklustre
I've been hit by more arrows
than General Custer

Six couplets in need of development

1. On confessional poetry

There are no skeletons in my cupboard
only strange foodstuffs I tend to hoard

2. On the subjective nature of empathy

Who really gives a toss
about the pain of a wasp?

3. On the racist who can speak so tenderly about the birth of a child

Even the most brutish
has a sense of honour and duty

4. On the difficulty of reality living up to over-sentimental
   expectations

Home is where the heart is
but two hours later and you're looking for an excuse to leave

5. On the redistribution of atoms and the repetition of history

Some breathe in Hitler
whilst others breathe a saviour

6. On the anticipation of regret

As soon as the flight leaves your fingertips
you know if the target is missed

On stepping out the door all past autumns inhaled

I wish I'd never before written a poem

I wish poetry itself had never even been conceived
that I could bring you a gift
unseen before God and the angels
like the formation of the very first star
or the first new born child on Earth

but this is not to be

Yet there is beauty in the formation of all new stars
though there are a million in the universe
and isn't each child that is born as precious as the first?

So I write this poem for you
in this way
because of poems I have written before

For even if I destroyed all my past attempts at poetry
it would be like trying to unlearn a language
or trying to forget the mechanics of walking
It is futile to romanticise naïvety and deny art and evolution

My first clumsy affairs were simple couplets
juvenilia full of basic mistakes

Later efforts showed promise but lacked true inspiration
Limericks with the ambitions of a sonnet

Once or twice favourable development
was spoilt by an untimely ending or
the breakdown of the sense of rhyme
It seems there are very few poems these days that endure

What I would really like to write is an epic
an all-time classic, a magnum opus
a life's work to be left unfinished

not the first or the last poem ever written but
a poem that would inspire all future generations
a poem that would outshine the brightest of stars
adorn the heavens and
leave even God and the angels breathless

This is the poem I would write for you

Jesus flies business class

On the airplane I saw Robert Powell
he who once played Jesus
So you'd think we'd be blessed with food less foul
than just clammy ham and cheeses

Did Francis of Assisi have the same rapport with insects?

He was the patron saint of animals
but what of the lowly insect?
Would a saint covered in cockroaches
be given the same respect?

Ode to the Trevi Fountain surrounded by scaffold

Love sick I may be
vino makes me maudlin
but even I couldn't write a song called
'3 coins on tarpaulin'

The mutually assured destruction of Mr and Mrs Jones

Like in most arguments neither can remember
who fired the first shot
Both
still had snipers positioned from their previous confrontations
Both
had started to build entrenchments

This time though it had escalated
into open conflict on a scale never seen before
Mr Jones was flexing his muscles
Mr Jones was about to demonstrate who wore the trousers
Mrs Jones was beating the shit out of him

In the aftermath there followed a period of chilled silence
This Mr and Mrs Jones referred to as the Cold War
They built a wall between them
At first friends dropped in supplies

Each began developing new weapons to inflict pain upon the other
Each labelled their weapons 'deterrents'
Each was determined if need be
to 'deterrent' the other into oblivion

Then gradually
as paranoia became a firm enough basis to build upon
peace talks began

But if one day either of their tongues should slip...

Earlobes

Pendulous understated decoration
ripe for perforation
Why your creation
you superfluous elongation?

Utterly dispensable
your evolution nonsensical
Natural selection
seems to have overlooked correction
of your unwarranted projection

Is your lack of function
divine injunction
God's grin
at Darwin
making the origin
of the species
akin to a load of faeces?

Oh seductive appendage
Non-productive excess baggage

Have you purpose
or are you just fleshy surplus
An etc
without raison d'être?

Erroneous or purely erogenous?
Is there an answer to your dodginess?

Heaven sent or
hellish bent
oh cherished embellishment?

I have no quibble
only a desire to nibble
as you incite the cannibal

Why don't they teach you about mirrors at school?

Why do some people shy away from mirrors
or look up into mirrors fleetingly with pain on their brow?

Why do some people stare at mirrors in blank disbelief
questioning, anxious, searching, longing?

Why do some people cling to mirrors re-checking their stance
or prance like dolls playing out their expressions before mirrors?

Why do some people look long into mirrors at night
or in the quiet, praying for change

hoping to see that which isn't there, remembering what once was
fighting the image in the reflected mirror of their eyes?

The dream of the rood

Amid 60 million pieces of Heaven

some shapes appear so similar
but with 30 million two-piece jigsaws
it's not the easiest of puzzles

Worn and scuffed at the edges
the desperate and the unloved
force another faulty fit
hammering compromise into loose connections
distorting the surface to hide the ruptures beneath

> and always it seems the saddest feint
> the coward's selfish taunt at fate
> replacing love and hate with fixture
> painting over
> a mismatching picture

Foetus Madonna and child

Virgin birth without maternal consent
Product of a surgical rape by grave robbers
Conscripted icon to a mutilated God

...this is too impersonal

She has outgrown her parent from birth
An untidy addendum to Death's reckoning

A photo of an aborted foetus in a silver frame is no
compensation
Her nightmares would sicken even Mary Shelly

The scripture of chemical equations cannot comfort her
The strongest of nature's bonds eludes her

She could brush her grandmother in passing
and neither would ever know

The instruments of conception are kept immaculate
"Mother, I would breathe your name," she whispers

In sterile hands
she is no bigger than a donor card

Insider dealing

Stale air
is an insult to the gift of breath

the bite of life is an exquisite step

There is no season for 'lukewarm'
closeted from fields of white
numb
to the nuances of nature
and the bones of trees laced with ice

There are flowers that wilt in constant summer
There is a despair
        that kills more than the bleakest winter
Loud wallpaper
will never replace a lover's murmur

If only the saints would give birth
If only the smallest dreams came true
Maybe some night
when street lights enrapture the stars
and Heaven
comes down
to kiss the roofs

A belief in magic is no lack of respect
To wish
is but to brave the spirit's furthest edge

How the young and fashionable are feeling this season

They're wearing
their consciences well-hidden this season
Hearts on the sleeve are definitely out

Compassion's out
Basically the effect is not to distract attention
from the expensive clothes

Animate passion

Romance pales in the predictable

Now is
always the time for something irrational

Need

If need was currency
who could buy you
from me?

Hymn of the Madonna's hymen

There's nothing esoteric
about the holiest of relics
both scientists and clerics agree

though the inhibited regale
the glory of the Grail does pale
beside this symbol of female chastity

as do Christ's five foreskins
brought back from the crusades
the crown of thorns
and the centurion's blade

the cross and the bloodstained nails
even The Shroud of Turin fails
to grace the final blasphemy

The Madonna's hymen
once examined for semen
and traces of the holy ghost
by faithless men in clean white coats

in some laboratory enshrined
labelled for DNA
will sit
upon the shelf

until mankind
can find a way
to clone from it
God himself

Open graves

I saw my life on a library shelf today
tucked somewhere in between
Milton and Wilfred Owen

A very thin life it looked
A slim volume
A shallow grave

Exhumed only twice
Easily missed
but for the lack of dust, as yet

I worked my way backwards
Meredith, Marlow, MacDiarmid
These were lives to fill volumes

like headstones
memorials, mausoleums
shaming my pauper's grave

Standing back my life is lost
in the two dimensional
At a distance very few are discernible

Shakespeare
Now there was a substantial life
growing with each new century

Byron, Keats and Shelley
often found together
A bond of over fifteen decades

In time
with lack of space
making way for a new generation

my life displaced
may well fall open on this page
A page as thin as any death certificate

They've tried flushing
they've tried bleach
but it won't shift

They've tried scrubbing
with the little plastic brush
that matches the bath

They've even been reduced to
scouring on hands and knees
cursing their misfortune

It is never mentioned in conversation
It is ever between them
It is a guilt they share

They would move house
but for the prying of surveyors
They are looking for someone to blame

They are waiting for the other to depart

They leave the lid down
and feign problems with the plumbing
should people visit

Sun-slapped

I am a bright red panda
Personified Commie propaganda
A Ready Brek overdose
Medium-rare nettles on toast

The desert on fire
A blood-stained map of the old British Empire

A boiled alive crab
A human kebab
A raw snake
A Sellafield mistake

The Singing Detective
The stinging defective
Edam under the grill
Edamnation – a tattoo of Hell

Pompeii – the last day
A scolded X-ray
The Human Torch with backdraft
A rejected skin graft

Captain Scarlet on a spit
The DIY Atomic Bomb kit

A horror show in Braille
An acid attack on a scorpion's tail
A butcher's mess
As untouchable
as Eliot Ness

Sagrada Família (The Sacred Family)

Having spent twenty years or more
building a cathedral for the poor
I wonder if Gaudí said "Damn"
when he was run over by a tram

He left behind the world's largest folly
and a decorative effect
on the wheels of the trolley

Sex before parents

A parent expects
their son to have sex
but not so their daughter
true values they've taught her

But with their double standard logic
they never seem to have thought of
the fact their son sleeps around
with other parents' daughters

The whole woman

I have seen the Venus de Milo
and she is beautiful

Were her arms to be covering her modesty
or spread like a crucifix
beckoning like a lover
or hid away in submission?

In my naïvety
I am diminished by glib acceptance
Smarting from my own scars
I am left wanting

For then she spoke
and her voice was brave and true
and the figure became flesh
and the body became tender
and the whole woman was revealed
greater than the subtraction of parts
greater than my tourist imagination
could envisage

And as her words seduced my spirit
I was ashamed
how shallow had I been to accept
any less

I have seen the Venus de Milo
and she has spoken to me
and she is beautiful

The poet as a young girl

She's never come to terms with her shape
or been comfortable with any of her hairstyles

The clothes she hangs herself in never hold the person
she feels she wants to see in the mirror

No matter how she sits she feels awkward
She doesn't like the summer, it casts shadows on her face

She says her face is too angular that's the problem
Tight-fitting clothes make her feel disproportionate

Maybe she's getting old
she thinks

Pastimes

We pass the time between orgasms
with reassurance and affection
exploring the contours
drinking in the perfume
attentive

We pass the time between orgasms
with cups of coffee
short naps
toast
and maybe the crossword

We pass the time between orgasms
with days apart
work
sleep
routine

We pass the time between orgasms
with hobbies
and interests
escapes
and pastimes

The measuring of worth

No, my heart is not in competition
It does not beat out time racing others
It's not bigger or louder than others

I would not say all hearts should be like mine
or that my heart is of significance
Its only claim – it has come to exist

It is sometimes hard to hear your own heart
I've listened well to the hearts of others
and found some comfort in their tone and pulse

Here is the most intimate of murmurs
I offer as a tiny SOS
the warmth and persistence of my lifeblood

Merely the echoes of a human heart
yet perhaps reminiscent of your own

The poem within you

Opened to the chill of the room
is the poem deep inside you

You shrug and feign dismissal
but it is as you'd hoped
it is your poem

Private and sacred
it belongs to you alone

Guarded and enshrined
it is the very heart of you

You are concerned for its progress
You are both embarrassed and proud

and in an act of defiance
in an act of pure humanity
you hold out your poem
sure that it has its place

Opened to the chill of the room
is the poem deep inside you

and for a moment the room is warmed
and in that moment you are content

and in a world of such poems
how can anyone die lonely and cold?

Is there no room for miracles along the Bury road?

She has an Oscar

It is a small figure
standing upright
with arms wrapped
in front of its heart
clasping a sword

It is too small to be mistaken for a shrine

It is not a real Oscar obviously
merely a facsimile

From the stage though
it looks just like the real thing

It's not as heavy of course
so there is an element of pretence
needed to carry off the deception

This is called acting
and is the reason she was given the honour
in the first place

It is hollow
but there is no way moisture
could have fallen from its cheeks

Somewhere between interest and indulgence

There's so much trouble in the world
War, terrorism, oppression
world famine, earthquakes, poverty
and to top it all
I've got a cold sore

Ok so if all these things that happen are in God's plan
if it's all part of a great tapestry of human experience
how does my cold sore fit into all this?

We all have our crosses to bear only
I notice Jesus never had a cold sore

Perspective? How can I get things in perspective
when I've got a gigantic cold
sore obscuring my view?

Over-reacting? That's easy for you to say
you don't have to wake up with a huge monstrosity
threatening to obliterate your entire face

...Yes fine, it just burned itself out
Fickle, no it's not a question of fickle

By the way I see Argentina has invaded the Falklands
It was some time ago, I know that
I've been busy, I do have problems of my own you know

Lincoln Memorial

In Washington doth Lincoln sit
seemingly free of starling shit
If he was sat on Manhattan
his head would get shat on
unless he kept his hat on a bit

Mid-Wales crisis

My heart reminisces on a faster pace
like this seaside town in winter
but time and tide wait for no man
nor does the Aberystwyth sprinter

Middle-age spread

The eternal quest is but hassle
when in the test of youth
                                    you cannot compete
Five minutes on a bouncy castle
and five days smelling of deep heat

Did it rain on the first Good Friday?

A downpour of hailstones
on the way to the park
at any other time of year
would deter

It's Easter and the weatherman has egg on his face

Only kidding says the holy gaffer
his hazy grin
flashing like the amber
declaring All Fools' Day everyday

April is the time for prospecting illusions

for damp patches
getting the wind in your sails
constructing plans
two by two

for coming back from the dead
for fair weather friends to eat and run as

the umbrella and the parasol see-saw out and in doors
like neighbours trying to have the last word

Drizzle half-cocked
spring-loaded
Big G with an itchy trigger finger

Noah must have been a nervous wreck by the end
of April

The pious slug

If karma helps the soul progress
then what hope does the slug possess?

Can a slug exact the price
enact a virtue or a vice?

Do slugs have personality
or individuality?

Can a slug be good or evil
or be tempted by the Devil?

Can slugs have ambition or dreams
or hatch diabolical schemes?

Can slugs be morally punished?
How far can the soul be diminished?

She has never had a full-length mirror of her own

As a child she played make believe
in front of her mother's dresser

But now in her bedsit
all she has is a small bathroom unit set into the wall

The light is not flattering
and she is never drawn to check her reflection

Her new dresses
she never sees in full glory

It's no wonder she shies to the corners, arms crossed in front
and head lowered

Occasionally, in the midst of distraction, when out shopping
she will catch her reflection in a shop window

Occasionally
she'll linger those extra seconds thinking she could compete

Of course, she knows the glass is dark
and there is an element of distortion

Like with a telephone voice you have perfected a photo face

For this is

the self-conscious playing of you
the you the world at large is told to remember
the you with headlights on full beam at the oncoming traffic
the you to whom you feel you must aspire
the auditioning of you
the outside you
the heightened shell
the bold hoardings
the you without doubt or hesitation
the party you

None of your photos do you justice

Ostrich man

I can see no evil in the world
There's nothing can make me sad
I can't see anything because
my head's inside this bag

I'm not an animal I'm a man
I was given this by my dad
He said "One day everything you see will be yours"
then he gave me this bloody bag

The teachers gave me another
I got a further one from my mother
They gave me one at every job I had
They said "We can see a great future for you son
here, wear this very nice bag"

But now I'm dead they say I can take it off
but though they think I'm mad
I'll show them they can't discipline me
See, I'm still wearing my bag

Self-sufficient

In your dishonest silence you watch all exits
in case the logic of the big issues escape
and freedom becomes just another name for loneliness

The grass

is not only greener on the other side of the hill
it will
so they say
be greener tomorrow than it is today

Internal memo

Forget big business

the only holding company
I want
is you

The morning after pillow

Does love sleep?
or keep its favour
or cradle a nightmare
of a different colour

Hesitating in the middle distance
blocking the lane for the ambulance

Between the eroticism of detail
and an indefinite article

Devotion torn from the gift wrap
discolouring the hunger of stained glass

Like the inflatable globe that blows up in your face
Like the juggler trying to cover his fourth mistake

A blizzard of the heart
and the domino of principles

The domino of principles
and a blizzard of the heart

The 14th and 15th of February
are only an eyelid apart

The night my heart caught fire

The blue lights flashed like a cheap disco at a wedding
Six firemen in yellow hats and matching trousers
jumped out of the red engine and the hoses pissed forth

As damp rapidly became an understatement
a white hat took charge

"That's the worst case of heartburn I've ever seen," he joked
dragging me unconscious from the wreckage

When eventually I came to
I checked my inside pockets
I was in luck
they'd not wet my matches

The party to which you were not invited

was like no other party before
What a party
Everyone was there
Well, everyone, that is, but you

It was amazing
You wouldn't believe what went on
If you weren't at that party
then you don't know what party means

You just couldn't imagine a party like that
There'll never be a party like it again
Everyone's still talking about it
Well, everyone, that is, but you

A party like that can change your life
Let's face it any other party
is going to seem drab now in comparison
I mean, I've been to parties with a capital P

but this was a party with a capital P A R T Y
A party like that comes once in a lifetime
Still at least everyone can share the memory
Well, everyone, that is

Southern Cemetery

Like comic timing
old graves
bedded well in hard ground
sit easy in glib abstract

With assurance of place
haircuts grown out
beside mourners long since rejoined
our great grandfathers
surrender their individuality

In the grandeur of their anonymity
we grieve more for humanity
than our own mortality

Then we come upon God's latest crop
Fresh mounds of loose earth
soft like a hand on your brow
A scar still pink before the skin hardens

There's something disturbing
about the grouping of these
well-tended plots at the edge of the gate

The unweathered granite
the unworn epitaphs
like first year kids in their new uniforms
The soil as rich and brown as a new satchel

Anxious like their mother
we hesitate at the railings

On the far side of the high street
there's a choice of undertakers
and a discreet distance down the road
you can buy flowers

she felt more attractive already

The heart of a rabbit she used
to highlight her cheekbones

Her lips she smoothed with assorted rodents
Woodlice, cockroaches and other insects
darkened her lashes

Whilst the blinded eyes of labradors
she dabbed behind her ears

For the final touch
she slipped into a full-length mink

Turning to leave she
caught sight of her
reflection and squealed
with excitement

Tonight she was dressed to kill

The shoes worn by clowns are often too big
Real giants are rare amid
the sideshows of cowardice and guilt
the vain deception of dwarfs on stilts

Even
the gravestones of the famous eventually rot
The ashes of the tallest men
won't fill a small pisspot

Those passed have long outnumbered those bound
Every house is built on a cemetery
The Earth is all burial ground
washed by the souls of those lost at sea

And when God and Science have reckoned
in less
than a millionth of a second
all the atoms of the universe will be crammed in
to a space smaller than the head of a pin
There will be a huge explosion
and everything
will start all over again

Discovering your scent in the summer rain
Redefining a puddle as a small lake

The Glaisdale Schoolyard Alliance of 1974

At school
Valerie, Debby and Netta
were the best of friends

but you'd never see all three of them together
only ever two at a time
always having fallen out with the third

Val and Debby together
then Val and Netta
then Debby and Netta

At school Valerie, Debby and Netta
were the best of friends
They all hated Sandra Vickers

The enchantment of personality

In the original version
there were no real pirates and no hook
not in the physical sense
only the ominous ticking of a clock

And at the beginning of the story
Peter was just an ordinary boy
who living in a world without fairies
had become his own shadow
and it was he himself
who was trapped in the window

Funny how tales change in the telling
It was Wendy who was the heroine
She
it was
that saved him

She was the one who was magical
and when she giggled
as she often did
it was like the tinkling of a bell

This was her gift that could give the spirit wings
A gift that could free lost children
trapped in their grown-up clothes
and their responsible frowns

You see the original version
was not a fairy story at all
but a love story
for those that believe in such things

In defence of the moustache

It's unfair to sneer at selective facial hair
though it's hard to appear unassuming
with temperance towards near nasal grooming
Still, an untended upper lip follicle
is not inherently symbolical of anything diabolical

Ok Hitler was a fascist
and also a noted tash-ist
Stalin too was without dispute a
vicious persecutor
hirsute to boot below the hooter

However, though the tash on Hitler was littler
still Adolf did rate a greater dictator
proving the fallacy of this indicator

Mussolini was also rotten
but his top lip was as smooth as a baby's bottom

Nixon was bad though he had no
more than a five o'clock shadow
ipso facto QED, not bec'us he
had a mussy

For it is writ that it is craven
to mock the partially shaven

Though I wonder if the Bible
would have so many devotees
if the disciples
had all had goatees

You can go from Ian Botham to Desperate Dan
and it's easy to spot who's not
a full-blooded fan of Victor Kiam

If Jesus returns
will he sport Elvis sideburns?

A tribute to L.S. Lowry

The paintings of L.S. Lowry
could not be considered flowery
but then Salford city
is not very pretty
and more often than not it's showery

A tribute to Andy Warhol's wig

Andy Warhol was no mug
of him it can be said
he pulled the rug from under the Arts
and wore it on his head

Chelsea Hotel

As a tribute to Dylan Thomas
I got pissed at the Chelsea Hotel
and though the food was delicious
as a tribute to Sid Vicious
I threw up over the doorman as well

Why I'm against Christmas, New Year, birthdays and weekends

I'm against the prescription of placebo en masse

I'm against the misconception that jollity, jubilation
and generosity of spirit can be determined by timetable

I'm against the surrender of all individuality and free will
to a contrived agenda

I'm against peer pressure to emulate an idealised role model

I'm against forced obligations to suppress natural variations
in temperament

I'm against any corset on the emotions
emotional fascism and institutionalised social blackmail

I'm against the bland numbness of uniformity

I'm against denying the complexity of the human spirit
the allure of originality and the unique nature
of each human personality

I'm against the false promise that such moments
are of universal significance or in any way representative
of some longer set period

I'm against the inevitable repercussions of disappointment
and feelings of inadequacy inherently incurred

I'm against the arrogance of those converted
to the culture of the calendar which insists that all must bow
to this ritual or be chastised as if in some way lacking

The Acme God Company

Higher purchase with a higher purpose
Paradise privatized like a three ring circus

Heaven on high at down-to-Earth prices
Sell yourself right out of a crisis

Sell yourself something you already own
for the Father and the Son are just a family firm

and lo, the word of the Lord on the big board is quoted
as the Holy Spirit is finally floated

It's a preference share for Armageddon
See how the Dow Jones closes at Psalm one hundred and eleven

and behold the soul is sold from the National Health
so the poor that can't pay can go straight to Hell

and the Lord looked down on his Cherubim
lain broken on the ground with ruptured wings

and he wept

David Lawson's ego had grown enormously since he saw his work in print. He paraded his ego daily, took it for long walks. Sat it on his knee in the pub. It became his only topic of conversation.

At night he began to feed it with the odd passing acquaintance and very soon it developed a liking for flesh. Its appetite grew and not before long, old friends, distant relations and gradually complete strangers were ferociously attacked and left for dead.

Becoming uncontrollable, his ego enlarged with each victim it devoured. No longer were individuals enough, his ego began to challenge small groups; Tupperware parties, crochet clubs – easy meat. Stronger and stronger it became; now Rugby clubs and Kung Fu night classes fell victim. Not only third division football teams but their supporters as well, it assaulted en masse. Small northern towns it savaged without mercy. As his ego towered up to a giant fifty feet It began its attack on London, the Queen, the Armed Forces, Parliament and the Police, leaving them all devastated.

Brushing aside the Archbishop of Canterbury, the Pope and even Sir Cliff, the ego threw out a challenge to God himself. A fair fight the ego insisted. God remained silent. To limber up, the ego ransacked America and held up the blood of Hollywood. "Now," said the ego from the top of the Empire State Building, "send down the Four Horsemen of the Apocalypse and I'll tie one hand behind my back." Nothing happened.

"Ok God," threatened the ego, "I'm coming for you," and it leapt out into that great boxing ring in the sky. Four thousand feet later garbage men scraped the remains of David Lawson off the sidewalk.

"First round to me," said God.

"Low punch," the ego protested, biting hard on God's ankles.

Within minutes

She flings her arms around the world
as if to say "I love you, why won't you love me?"

Within minutes of meeting you
she'll have told you her entire life story
she'll have squeezed your arm
she'll have bought you a drink

She sees all her own faults but no-one else's
she needs constant reassurance
she finds relationships never last but
she's never the one to break up; no matter what

she clings on and clings on tight
as if to say "I love you, why won't you love me?"

Sorry

'Sorry' is a small word only five letters
that is four different letters and one swap
having two letter 'r's

'I love you' is three small words
eight letters, that is seven and one swap
the letter 'o'

'I forgive you' is two small words and a fairly
small word, eleven letters, ten and one swap

I'll exchange you one of my most valuable 'sorry's
and an almost priceless 'I love you'
that's thirteen letters in all
if you exchange one 'I forgive you'

Of course, if you want to throw in an 'I love you too'
we can really start talking business

Donkey and the old maid

Guilt
Resentment
Unfulfilled ambition
Jealousy...

"The complete set
Happy Family!"
declared the husband
laying his cards on the table

"Happy Family?" puzzled the wife
"I thought we were playing snap"

Natasia

I loved Natasia
after a fashion
and she could have loved me truly
if only after
a night of passion
I hadn't called her Julie

Confessions of a closet celibate

Now lust can rust 'cos I'm bored of sex
My libido's just a place where dust collects

You know the first signs of tedium are on their way
when you actually start snoring during foreplay

Then you can bemoan your hormones as really down the pan
when each orgasm seems like a predictable rhyme that takes too
long to attain
                        and doesn't quite scan

Once a drug upon which I thrived

now the insertion of protruding bits of the anatomy into the
anatomy of another to effect a momentary sensation of pleasure
together with a short period of wellbeing all seems somewhat
                        too contrived

Where once during sex
to prolong the climax
I would go through the names of all the teams in the Premier League
                        and mentally record them

now I do the same with the Championship
purely to prevent boredom

Exaggerated thoughts about an internal bruise

There's a figure taken to sitting on my bed at night
I've asked him if he's me and he says he thinks not

I've asked him what he symbolises
and he says he's not sure he symbolises anything

I've asked him what he's doing there
and he says he's been wondering that himself

I've asked him if he knows how long he plans to stop
and he says it's difficult to make any plans when you only
exist intermittently and in another's imagination at that

I've asked him if he's one of those ominous dark brooding
shadows that appear in poetry purporting to be deep and
meaningful but he just looked at me in disbelief
and said he bloody hoped not

My girlfriend refuses to discuss him
She's never seen him
He's never there when she stops

He was there once when I lived with my old girlfriend
but we broke up a week later

I remember first seeing him when I was about ten or eleven
Around Christmas time
Of course, he was a lot younger then

He mostly confines himself to the bedroom
Although I have seen him once or twice
out of the corner of my eye sat on the bus

And last summer I could have sworn he was following me
everywhere I walked

There's not a lot more to say about him really
He keeps himself to himself
He tries very hard not to appear ominous
and gets quite embarrassed if you mention it

Reduced to reading the spines on bookshelves at parties

She wore her monogamy like
a thermal vest

She found identity only in coupling
Felt happiness only by proxy

When he left
she lay discarded like a single glove

Self-conscious like a birthday guest
arriving without a present

Let's pretend

Let's pretend we're both drunk and you're not married
and I'm not courting that girl in the kitchen and nobody
can see us and we don't know what we're doing and you put
your hand down my trousers whilst I lick your nipples and
if anyone comes in and finds us we were only pretending

And because it's dark we can pretend to fumble about and
grope at each other's crotch and buttocks and you can drape
your knickers over my head whilst I bend you over the chair
and if people should say anything we can pretend it was only
innocent party games and when we sink to the ash-stained
carpet exhausted and unkempt we can pretend it was great and
even that we share something special and then you can go back
to your husband and I to my girlfriend and pretend

The uncommon touch

If life imitated art
I would write a poem called
'If life imitated art'
and this would be its start

And I would read it out at a performance
pretending it was satirical
and just exploring a poetic device
but courting disaster

My desperation like a half rhyme
I would try to disguise
hoping that fate
could so easily be mastered

During the poem
a woman I have never spoken to before
would recognise the desperation in my voice
as her own

She may or may not be attractive
but when she approaches me after the show
I am captivated by her presence

We talk casually passing the moments
but there is a hesitation born through longing
and all distractions blur from vision

Feigning the context of coincidence
we arrange to meet up the next day
It is sunny
and there is no awkwardness in our greeting

As twenty years melt away
we can still remember each shortened breath of this day
and all distractions blur from vision

but
and this is the but of a cynic
life will only imitate art tonight
if the poem I write will be met
with a degree of embarrassed fidgeting
and murmurs of 'self-indulgent and love sick'
degenerating into general confusion
when it fails to end with a display of wit

and maybe even annoyance by some
who'd not really paid to see this kind of stuff
and later after the fact
people will avoid eye contact
especially those that recognise desperation
especially those that recognise their own desperation

and I will go home
and I will think up another poem
to help break through these barriers trying
to achieve the control in art
that is impossible in life

knowing that I
would give away all my writing if life
imitated art and I could have put
a full stop to this poem
before the word 'but'

The problem with metaphor

Would Robert the Bruce
have bumped his head
half-pissed on Woodpecker cider

if on the wall of the cave
he'd watched instead
a daddy-longlegs not a spider?

Titian a bag

If Titian was painting today
think of the money he'd make
by picturing his nudes reclining
eating a Cadbury's Flake

The genius of Michelangelo

When sculpting 'the perfect man'
the real insight of the job
was making David's head too big
in proportion to the size of his knob

Undressing for sex when you feel you're getting fat

It's easy to tell if someone's self-conscious about being
overweight
because when they undress for sex
they always take their trousers off
before their shirt

Another dead giveaway
is the futile attempt
to hold their stomach in
whilst trying to pull off their socks

With practise what usually happens is this –
firstly they make a bee-line
for the side of the bed
away from the bedside lamp

Then back turned to both the light and their partner
they slip down their trousers past their knees
whilst at the same time lowering themselves
into the upright sitting position on the edge of the bed

Next they step out of the trouser legs
tread off their socks, undo all their shirt buttons
breathe in and try in one swift movement
to discard their shirt and slip gracefully under the cover

A complete waste of effort
No-one but no-one
has a hope in Hell of ever enjoying sex
whilst trying to hold their breath

Blinking

1.
I'm listening to the barber through a mirror
conversing like a photocopier selling minor revelations of a
personal nature

2.
Underground people are hanging from the ceiling like piglets
from a sow
whilst biorhythms linked into the Dow Jones take a bow

3.
Somewhere without question
lovers are praying to the pace of a botanical garden

4.
The man in the chair next
refracts a glib eye over a woman's breast

    This is the relativity of Franken Truth
    like four photos in a photo booth

"£49.90," said the man with the clipboard
"A full refund, sign here."

"I don't understand," I said, "refund on what?"

"£49.90, that's the total as far as our records show," he explained.
"We don't go back beyond decimalization. Wishes made before
that date come under a separate department."

"I see," I muttered, still not understanding, "did you say wishes?"

He tapped his pencil impatiently. "It's all fully itemised, wishing
wells, fountains, even the twenty pence you once tossed into a
canal pretending it to be magical, all refundable, just sign here."

"But I had hoped some day the wishes might..." I began

He took a closer look at his clipboard and shook his head

"I wasn't really expecting," I said feeling the need for some excuse,
"I was just hoping."

"£49.90," he offered

"It's not the money," I said, "I was just hoping... I was just—"

"Do you want the refund or not?" he insisted, "I've got many
more people to see."

"I don't think I'll sign," I said

He made a note on his clipboard and turning to go he grumbled,
"Just once I'd like to get a signature, just once."

Waiting for loco

My love
her beauty never pales
for her I'll wait
                forever

My love
she comes by British Rail
so better late
                than never

The trainspotter of love

She was sophistication personified
an angel with hazel eyes
unmoved by my yearning
to my passion burning
        her indifference would not yield
as the train stopped
my hopes dropped
        and she got off at Macclesfield

The black hole that was Phillip Mitchell

Phillip Mitchell had been depressed for some time – aeons in fact. But it came as something of a surprise to both astronomers and to his mother alike when, during a solar eclipse, Phillip Mitchell imploded.

His mother thought nothing of it at first; Phillip was always seeking attention and she felt this was just another of his little tricks. "The universe doesn't revolve around you Phillip," she would often remark.

Even when cutlery started to go missing she refused to accept that her own son was any different from every other crazy mixed-up teenager. "It's something he'll grow out of," she told Patrick Moore on a *Sky at Night* special.

Not until the back bedroom and most of the upstairs landing had mysteriously disappeared did Mrs Mitchell concede that Phillip needed guidance.

Several doctors were consulted but all were sucked into the abyss, as was the remainder of the house, the topsoil of the back garden and Mr Pollock's garage.

Specialists were called in but the problem was now out of hand. Most of Greater Manchester had already vanished.

Scientists worked around the clock. All military forces were mobilised. Panic gripped the Earth.

Within days the whole of the Northern Hemisphere was no more. In less than a week all traces of the Earth had disappeared.

The moon quickly followed, as did the other planets in the solar system and even the sun itself.

One by one the stars in the Milky Way were devoured until, eventually, galaxies from the furthest reaches were dragged inward.

Soon the entire universe was void.

"That'll teach them," said Phillip, sucking in the nothingness.

Cardigans to the Middle East

I have a dream
of a world without armies
A world of peace
where everyone wears cardies

Attack is ONLY the best defence
for those who lack sartorial elegance
It creates an impression to lessen aggression

Hooligans with lager cans
are never dressed in cardigans
Dr Who in his TARDIS
was never invaded by Daleks in cardies

You never see a pit bull
in a nice bit of wool
Attila the Hun
never wore a cardigan

The Marquis de Sade he
never wore a cardy
John Terry wouldn't be such a hard man
if he had to play in a cardigan

Better than a sweater or a bulletproof vest
you never see a cardy in battle dress
The UN troops would make proper guardians
If they swapped their berets for light blue cardigans

This paragon of haute couture
could ensure an end to war
So strengthen your defences
with Marks and Spencer's

I have a dream on behalf of man
where the symbol of peace and love
is a white dove
in a cardigan

The moon declares not its age but its beauty

Though bureaucrats
schedule scorn within their petty margins
and though tomorrow
seems as distant
as the furthest of God's silhouettes

giddy
to the moment shared
Time
is a child running rings in a garden
and the moon declares not its age but its beauty

She inflicted her love like a wound

and only when it wept did she have faith in it
It was a love that cowered in doorways
a love that talked in accusations

Where the words 'I love you' became a threat
and where love hung like terror
over every chance remark

Fossils on computer

Permanence itself is a temporary illusion

It is impossible to stand perfectly still
for any sustained length of time

Muscles tire and strain
Even the most determined
are beaten

Flowers bloom and wither
and new shoots emerge in their place
not the exact same petals
but no less beautiful

The weather changes hour to hour
day to day, season to season
and rain falls
never the exact same droplets
but no less fluid

There is nothing since creation
unchanged
stars disperse and reform
distances lengthen
the universe is reborn each instant
but is no less miraculous

The Mercurian love poems

Now no time   love poems
Wrap   pages   your arms
Across   blisters

God   good, we   together

Try not swallow   too often
    lend you   shadow,   must dig

See   leg bleed
Smear   blood   your face

    must not
   cry again
     so soon

Lay beneath   body   is moisture lost to   ground

    would touch   but for   pain

These   only words, let   breath cool face

When   happens   must not give up

Stretch   over you, wear me like   outer skin

The last poem I ever wrote

The last poem I ever wrote I had such high hopes for

The last poem I ever wrote was to have been so powerful
it would make war obsolete and eradicate poverty
even back through time

It was to have been so cleverly constructed
it would hold the key to the very universe itself
explain reality and even reveal the nature of God

So full of life it would be strapped onto wounds
and made into tablets and ointment

The Olympic Committee would disqualify competitors
found to have read it

Laid over the face of a corpse it would bring the dead back to life

The last poem I ever wrote was published
in a low budget poetry magazine boasting a print run of 220
150 of which still remain under the editor's bed

The title escapes me but it was some pathetic pun such as *Write Now*

The last poem I ever wrote was performed
to an alternative cabaret audience at Cleethorpes
off-season
in between an alternative juggler
and a 22-piece Catalonian dance band

Coinciding with the call for last orders
it was heckled constantly by a drunk born and bred in London
who sang in a Scotch accent
and claimed to own the city of Glasgow personally

The last poem I ever wrote was entered in a poetry competition
by a lifelong enemy

The judges, having been certified dead, were suitably appointed
as their names were unknown even to each other
let alone to anyone else

My poem came 63rd out of 7 million entries
and won a year's subscription
to the *Crumpsall Poetry Appreciation Society Crochet Circle and
    Glee Club Gazette*

The last poem I ever wrote was cremated along with my body
unread
The last poem I ever wrote was carried in the hearts
of those I loved